Kittens

★ A very first picture book ★

The original publishers would like to thank the North London Shelter of the Cat's Protection League for supplying the kittens who appear in this book.

For a free color catalog describing Gareth Stevens Publishing's list of high-quality books and multimedia programs, call 1-800-542-2595 (USA) or 1-800-461-9120 (Canada). Gareth Stevens Publishing's Fax: (414) 225-0377.

Library of Congress Cataloging-in-Publication Data

Kittens: a very first picture book / consultant, Nicola Tuxworth.
     p. cm. — (Pictures and words)
   Includes bibliographical references and index.
   Summary: Photographs and simple text present kittens engaged in a variety of activities.
   ISBN 0-8368-2273-0 (lib. bdg.)
   1. Kittens—Juvenile fiction. [1. Cats—Fiction. 2. Animals—Infancy—Fiction.] I. Title. II. Series.
PZ10.3.K6426   1999
[E]—dc21   98-31776

This North American edition first published in 1999 by
Gareth Stevens Publishing
1555 North RiverCenter Drive, Suite 201
Milwaukee, WI 53212 USA

Original edition © 1996 by Anness Publishing Limited. First published in 1996 by Lorenz Books, an imprint of Anness Publishing Inc., New York, New York. This U.S. edition © 1999 by Gareth Stevens, Inc. Additional end matter © 1999 by Gareth Stevens, Inc.

Senior editor: Sue Grabham
Editor: Sophie Warne
Photography: Lucy Tizard
Design and typesetting: Michael Leaman Design Partnership

Picture credits: Solitaire Photographic/Angela Rixon: pp. 8-9, 20-21.

Printed in Mexico

1 2 3 4 5 6 7 8 9 03 02 01 00 99

Kittens

★ A very first picture book ★

Nicola Tuxworth

Gareth Stevens Publishing
MILWAUKEE

Let's play
tag.

You can't
catch me!

What's
this?

6

Got it
this time!

I can see you ...

... and I'm going to
get you! I'm
a spotted leopard
in the jungle.

Mmm...
What's this?

It smells
nice.

10

Can I eat it?

We're really
hungry.

Wait for
me!

There's lunch.
Let's go!

Now for a bath ...

... and a
scratch.

That
was a
nice
nap.

I'm sure
that
wasn't
there
before ...

I'd better investigate.

I wonder
what this
is for?

Can I
climb *up*
it ...

... or *through* it?

What a busy day
we've had.

It's time
for bed.

It's a new day, so
look out, here I come!

Questions for Discussion

1. Can you name some of the "big cats" that live in the wild? How is a big cat, such as a lion, similar to the kittens shown in this book? How is it different?

2. How does a mother cat take care of her kittens? How would you take care of a kitten? What would you feed it? Would you take it to the veterinarian?

3. What words can you think of to describe the kittens in this book?

4. What kinds of toys do kittens like? Why do you think they like them?

5. How does a kitten use its senses to explore and learn about the world? Should kittens and cats be allowed to play outside? Why not?

More Books to Read

Buster and the Little Kitten. Hisako Madokoro (Gareth Stevens)

Cats. Animals Are Not Like Us (series). Graham Meadows (Gareth Stevens)

House Pets. Animals at a Glance (series). Isabella Dudek (Gareth Stevens)

The Kitten Book. Camilla Jessel (Candlewick Press)

Mitzi, Molly, and Max the Kittens. Real Baby Animals (series). Gisela & Siegfried Buck (Gareth Stevens)

Where's My Kitten? Michele Coxon (Puffin Books)

Videos

The Cat. (Barr Films)

Just Call Me Kitty. (Unicom Video)

Kitten Companions. (Northstar Entertainment)

Kitty Love! (Capital Cities/ABC Video Publishing)

Pets: A First Film. (Phoenix/BFA)

Web Sites

www.catlovers.com

www.bestfriends.org

Some web sites stay current longer than others. For further web sites, use your search engines to locate the following topics: *felines, humane society, jungle cats, kittens, leopards, lions, pumas,* and *wildcats.*

Glossary-Index

catch: to get hold of something that is moving. (p. 5)

climb: to travel upward on something, such as a ladder or hill. (p. 18)

hungry: wanting or needing food. (p. 12)

investigate: to look into something closely to learn more about it. (p. 17)

jungle: a tropical place with lots of trees, vines, and other plants. (p. 9)

leopard: a large wildcat from Africa that has a light brown coat with black spots. (p. 9)

spotted: covered with dots or patches of color. (p. 9)

wonder: to think about something. (p. 18)

27 JUN 2000

DEMCO